Praise for A Simple Way to Understand Every.......

A Simple Way to Understand Everything, by psychologist Mike Gobel, taps into the diverse fields of mathematics, philosophy, psychology, counseling and spirituality. The title is ambitious, but the layout of the book is compact and direct. The author uses an accessible style and invites the reader to embrace a transactional approach of child/parent/adult when considering personal reactivity and living in the real world. This being a short and concise book, it is not scientific or research oriented. It is not footnote verified. Gobel seems to have come to his written summations through the synthesis of his own reading, studying, counseling and interaction with those in his world sphere. He invites the reader into a world of their own contemplation and discovery through a variety of personal exercises that conclude each chapter. He suggests you are not broken or less than whole. You need to find your way back home through a somewhat foggy field of remembering. It is a short book and an easy re-read, allowing you to focus on key points and repeat helpful exercises. Wholeness is just down the pathway of remembering and integrating.

— Timothy Nickel, Hospice Chaplain

Praise for Living Cosmic Me Program

I've done a lot of personal growth work prior to joining Mike on the Living Cosmic Me journey. I found that the process gave me new things to think about and that I discovered ways of naming and understanding ideas and concepts that had begun to stir for me; they grew and became more vital during the Modules and the individual coaching time. Mike is a great listener and is able to provide safe space for exploring your own potential. I highly recommend you for trying Living Cosmic Me!

-- Rev. Dr. Kathy Harvey Nelson, Director, The Center for Spiritual Formation

Published: 2025, Author: Michael Patrick Gobel, 1st Edition, ISBN# 979-8-9992467-0-7

Publisher: Living Cosmic Press

Website: LivingCosmicMe.com

Simple Way to Understand Everything:

The Heartfelt Geometry of Self-Love, Wholeness, and Harmonic Service

Introduction

We are not broken. We are remembering.

This book was not written to fix you. It was written to reflect
you. It offers a simple, compassionate framework for
understanding the complex, often overwhelming experience of
being human— especially now, in a time of rapid spiritual
awakening, emotional excavation, and social transformation.

You may be someone who has always longed to help others, to
bring light, love, or healing into the world. Or you may simply
be someone who has struggled to make sense of your own
inner life— your emotions, your relationships, your patterns of
self-criticism or exhaustion. Wherever you are, this book meets
you there.

Rooted in over fifty years of experience in the fields of
counseling, emotional healing, and spiritual exploration, the
model presented here integrates the timeless wisdom of
psychology with the expansive lens of spiritual wholeness. It
distills everything into three primary aspects of being:

- The **Inner Child**, who feels
- The **Inner Parent**, who believes
- The **Inner Adult**, who chooses

When these three aspects are aligned and honored—not judged or suppressed—they create a harmonic inner space from which all healing, creation, and service naturally flow. This is the geometry of coherence. This is the simple way.

This book is also a seedbed for something larger: the *Living Cosmic Me* program, a self-guided pathway toward stabilizing your own energetic field, embodying your soul's presence, and serving others from overflow rather than depletion. But whether you take this journey alone, in community, or as part of a formal program, the core principles remain the same:

You are enough. You are whole. You are already the medicine.

Let's begin the remembering—together.

~

About the Author

I have always been a mirror—first for the pain of others, and now for their wholeness.

For decades, I walked beside others through their grief, trauma, longing, and self-doubt. I held space. I listened. I tried to fix and help and heal. And through that sacred labor, I slowly began to meet myself—not as a role, not as a helper, but as a presence. As breath. As being.

This book is not a theory. It is a transmission—a field reflection of my own journey from external service to internal coherence. From rescuing to resonance. From striving to simply stabilizing.

My formal background includes extensive training in counseling, psychotherapy, and spiritual mentorship. But what shaped me most were the moments of stillness: the times I allowed myself to feel the ache of my own unloved places, and let them be held by something greater.

I offer this book not as an expert, but as a fellow traveler. One who has lived through the question: *Is there a simple way to understand everything?* And who now offers an answer—not final, but harmonic:

Yes. And it begins with remembering who you are.

Welcome.

Table of Contents

Chapter 1 – The Pattern Beneath Everything

Opening the Field *(Geometry Lens)*

There is a pattern beneath everything you see.
It is not visible to the eyes in the way a tree or a river is
visible — yet it shapes the way the tree grows and the river
bends.
It is the quiet geometry of life, holding everything in a
precise harmony that is far from random.

We live inside this pattern every moment, whether we
know it or not.
When we are aligned with it, life feels as if it moves with
us.
When we drift away from it, we feel the tension of
swimming against a current we cannot name.

This is not about control.
It is about relationship — the way a sail listens for the
wind,
the way a bird tilts its wings to ride the unseen air.

Making It Human *(Psychology Lens)*

In psychological terms, this pattern shows up as the interplay between your thoughts, emotions, and behaviors. We often think of them as separate, but they form a self-reinforcing loop — a living system.
Your thoughts create emotional responses.
Those emotions shape the actions you take.
Your actions reinforce the original thoughts.

If the loop is rooted in fear, you will tend to find confirming evidence that the world is unsafe.
If the loop is rooted in trust, you will see opportunities and connections where others see only obstacles.

Most people don't notice the loop because they are inside it.
They take it to be "reality" rather than "a patterned way of seeing reality."
But once you learn to notice it, you can step back and begin to work with it instead of being ruled by it.

The Meeting Point

This is where the Geometry and the Psychology meet.
The inner loops of thought and feeling are not separate
from the larger patterns of the field.
They are micro-expressions of the same universal
geometry.
The way you hold your inner world shapes how the larger
pattern meets you.

In geometry terms:
You are a resonance point in the field.
The clearer and more coherent your resonance, the more
the field responds in harmony.

In psychological terms:
You are a meaning-maker.
The stories you tell yourself about life shape the way you
perceive and engage with it — and that perception subtly
organizes what you experience next.

Alignment as a Living Practice

Alignment is not a single moment of insight.
It is an ongoing practice of adjusting, like tuning a stringed
instrument or steering a small boat.
Some days the tuning comes easily.
Other days it feels as though the wind is against you.

From the Geometry Lens:
You are listening for the subtle harmonics that tell you
when you are in phase with the larger pattern.

From the Psychology Lens:
You are developing awareness of your own patterns of
thought, emotion, and behavior — noticing where they are
congruent with your deeper values and where they are not.

Both lenses point to the same truth:
Life flows best when you are internally coherent.
That coherence radiates outward, influencing not only your
own experience but the field you are part of.

Why This Matters

When you live in this way — attuned to both the unseen
geometry and the tangible psychology of your life —
you begin to feel a subtle shift:

- Life feels less random.
- Challenges become invitations.
- Other people respond to you differently, even if
  they don't know why.

The point is not to live without difficulty.
The point is to live with a felt sense of connection — to
yourself, to others, and to the larger intelligence that holds
us all.

An Invitation

You do not have to master both lenses to begin.
You only have to be willing to notice:

- How your inner patterns are mirrored in your outer life.
- How small shifts in your awareness and self-story can change the quality of your days.

This book will invite you to explore both lenses together.
You will see how the same truth can be understood as a pattern in the field and as a pattern in the psyche —
and how working with both gives you more than the sum of either alone.

So, as we begin, take a moment to imagine that your life is not happening *to* you, but *for* you.

After you begin to see that life is happening for you, it shifts and you see that it is happening with you.

That the geometry beneath everything is not a distant abstraction,
but a living companion —
and that your psychology is not an obstacle to spirit,
but one of the most direct pathways into it.

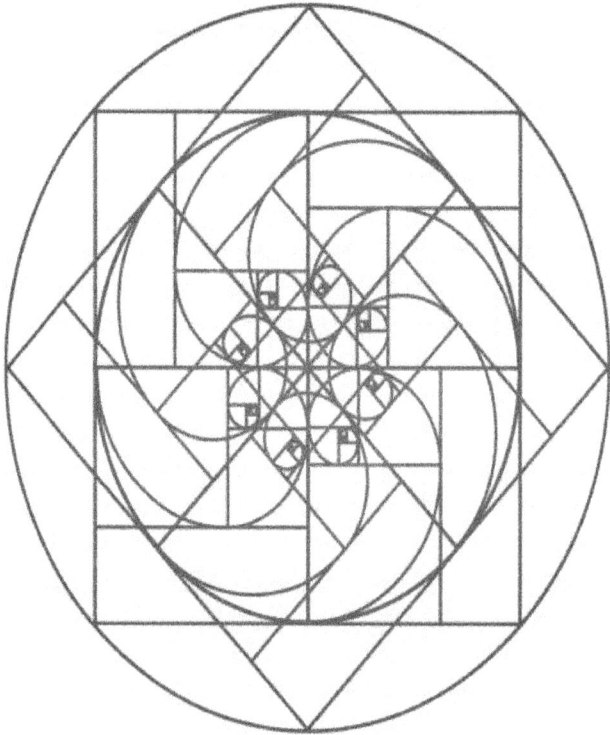

Chapter 2 – Life Is Happening For You
Opening the Field *(Geometry Lens)*

Life is not happening *to* you as much as it is happening *for* you.
It is an ongoing conversation between your inner world and the greater field you live in.

Everything you encounter — each person you meet, each circumstance you face — carries a frequency.
That frequency interacts with your own.
It is as if the field is holding up mirrors in many shapes and sizes, inviting you to see what is happening inside you.

From the Geometry Lens, these are **resonance events**.
The field is not random.
It is a coherent pattern, always matching what is unspoken within you.
Your inner state is not a private island.
It is woven into the whole, and the whole responds to you accordingly.

Making It Human *(Psychology Lens)*

Psychologically, this is easier to understand if you think in terms of cause and effect — but with a twist.
Your mind doesn't just respond to life; it shapes what you notice, how you interpret it, and the meaning you give it.

If you feel unworthy, you are more likely to notice situations that confirm that belief.
If you feel capable and loved, you'll recognize opportunities and support more quickly.
It's not that the outer world has changed — it's that your inner state is filtering and interpreting it in a particular way.

Life events often act like prompts — cues that bring your attention to a certain place.
Someone may irritate you, and you think the problem is "out there," but often it's pointing toward an old wound or unexamined belief inside you.
If you're willing to see it, the outer world becomes a feedback system for your inner growth.

The Dance Between Inner and Outer

From the Geometry Lens:
The outer is a reflection of the inner, the way a wave is a reflection of the wind that shapes it.
Energy expresses itself in patterns.
If you hold a pattern of trust, the field meets you in trust.
If you hold a pattern of fear, the field mirrors fear.

From the Psychology Lens:
We see this as cognitive-emotional feedback loops.
Your beliefs create emotional states, which shape your behavior, which reinforces your beliefs.
Life gives you situations that match the emotional "tone" you're carrying, reinforcing your inner world until you shift it consciously.

Why the Prompts Are a Gift

This is why I say life is happening *for* you.
The situations you face are not punishments or rewards —
they are information.
They are invitations to notice what you are carrying inside,
because what you carry inside shapes the world you
experience.

The field is not against you.
It is not indifferent to you.
It is, in a sense, collaborating with you — offering
reflections so you can see more clearly.
Every prompt, whether pleasant or painful, is part of your
larger becoming.

A Practice for Awareness

You can begin simply:
When something in your day triggers you — frustration,
sadness, defensiveness, even joy — pause.
Ask yourself:

- *What is this showing me about what I'm holding inside?*
- *What belief or emotion does this connect to?*

- *If I could shift my inner tone here, how might my outer experience change?*

From the Geometry Lens:
You are listening for resonance — the vibration beneath the event.
From the Psychology Lens:
You are becoming aware of your cognitive-emotional filters and making them conscious.

Closing the Loop

As you practice, you will notice a shift.
You begin to feel less like life is "happening to you" and more like you are in a **living dialogue** with it.
The outside still has challenges, but they no longer feel like random intrusions.
They feel like part of the work you came here to do — and part of the joy of being alive.

When you start to see life this way, the prompts become less threatening.
You can meet them with curiosity instead of judgment.
And that curiosity is where transformation begins.

Chapter 3 – The Power of Choice
The Geometry of Choice

In the great design of things, choice is not random.
It is one of the most potent tools encoded into the pattern of human experience.

From the Geometry Lens, choice is a **vector** — a directional point that influences resonance.
Every time you choose — not just externally, but inwardly — you shift your energetic alignment.
You change the frequency you emit, which changes what echoes back from the field.

From this perspective, **choice is creative**.
It is how you sculpt your field from the inside out.

You are never just reacting to the world.
You are participating in it — adjusting your frequency, shaping your experience with every decision, no matter how small.

The Psychology of Choice

From the Psychological Lens, we often think of choice as willpower:
Should I do this or that? Should I speak or stay silent?

But beneath that is something more powerful:
Awareness of pattern.

If you can pause long enough to recognize:

- *Why* you're leaning toward one action over another,

- *What emotion or thought is driving you?*
- And *whether that pattern is familiar or new…*

…you move from automatic behavior to conscious authorship.

Most human suffering arises not from the absence of choice, but from the **absence of awareness** in the moment when a choice was available.

We choose by default what is most familiar — until we learn to choose what is most **aligned.**

Two Lenses, One Moment

Let's imagine you're triggered by something — a comment, a look, a delay.
Old anger flares. Part of you feels young, reactive, unseen.
In that moment, it seems like **you have no choice** — just a rush of emotion and an instinct to protect or push away.

But wait.

In Geometry terms:
You're standing at a **fork in the field**.
Two pathways vibrate in front of you: one that loops you back into the old frequency, and one that opens a new harmonic.

In Psychology terms:
You are witnessing a **split between conditioned reaction and conscious presence**.
The "inner child" may want to speak, the "parent" may judge, the "adult" may notice both and ask:
What's actually happening here?

This is the moment of choice.

It is subtle.
But it is powerful enough to change the trajectory of your life.

Choice as Field-Shaping

You don't need to change the world in a day.
But with each conscious choice, you change
your **relationship to the world** — and the world responds.

Geometry:
A single tone, slightly adjusted, alters the whole harmonic.

Psychology:
A single reframed thought, slightly softened, shifts your emotion, your behavior, your pattern.

And the beauty is — once this happens enough times,
the **new pattern becomes the default**.
You're not just choosing differently.
You're *becoming* someone who resonates differently.

A Practice: The Pause Between

Try this:

1. When you notice a reaction rising — pause.
2. Ask yourself:
   - *What am I feeling?*
   - *What old story does this connect to?*
   - *Is there a more aligned response available to me now?*
3. Wait for the inner tone to soften or shift.
4. From that place — choose.

You are not looking for perfection.
You are listening for **coherence**.

The power is not in having every answer.
The power is in **remembering that you get to choose which field you inhabit**.

Closing Reflection

Choice is not about control.
It's about remembering you are not just a product of what has happened to you —
You are a living response to it.

And when you choose from a place of inner alignment, you activate something ancient and divine within you.

You become a tuning fork for truth.

And that changes everything.

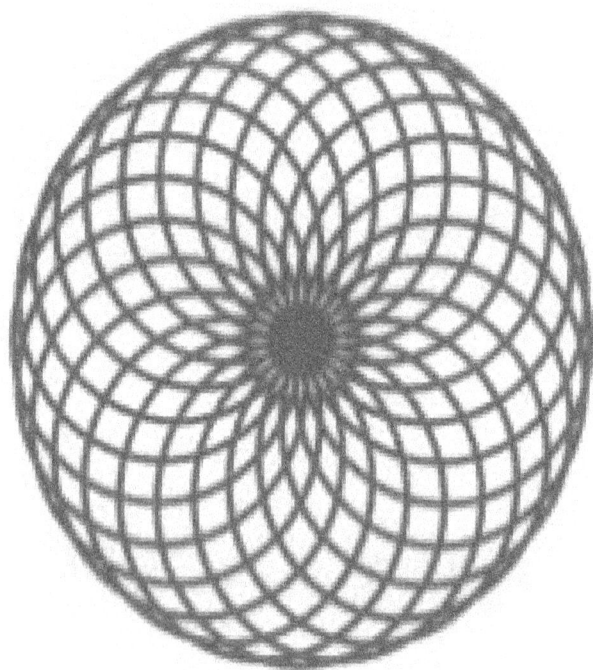

Chapter 4 – The Inner Architecture: Who's Speaking?

Geometry Lens: Nested Fields Within a Field

Within you are many voices — not random, but nested.
Like concentric circles or the layered spirals of a seashell,
your inner landscape is composed of distinct energetic
patterns, each with its own resonance and function.

Some parts of you feel young.
Some sound like your mother.
Others are still discovering how to speak.

In Geometry terms:
You are a constellation of subfields — each part vibrating
at its own frequency, yet all contained within the singular
field of your being.
When these parts are aligned, your life flows.
When they pull in different directions, the field distorts —
and so does your experience.

Psychology Lens: The Three-in-One Model

In psychology, this internal constellation is often described
using parts work or ego-state models.
My own framing is simple and effective:
You carry within you three primary voices:

1. **The Inner Child** – Feeling-based, sensitive, reactive, present.
2. **The Internal Parent** – Judgment-based, controlling, shaped by the past.
3. **The Conscious Adult** – Observing, integrating, and choosing with awareness.

This is not a theory.
It's how the psyche organizes itself — especially when under stress.

When the Voices Clash

When your child part is triggered — afraid, hurt, overwhelmed — it often activates the inner parent.
The parent rushes in with rules, shame, or a lecture.
It sounds like control, but underneath is fear:
What if we fall apart? What if we're not okay?

Meanwhile, the adult voice — your presence, your clarity — gets drowned out.

You say or do something you later regret.
Or you freeze, unable to decide.
You feel confused, anxious, torn between two directions.

From the Geometry perspective:
This is **frequency interference**.
Multiple subfields are emitting incoherent signals.
The field becomes tangled, and life reflects that back to you.

From the Psychological perspective:
This is **internal misalignment**.

Unintegrated parts are reacting to past wounding, not present reality.

The Role of the Conscious Adult

Healing begins when the Conscious Adult steps forward.
This part of you doesn't fix, control, or override.
It *witnesses*. It *listens*. It *loves*.

The adult is the tuning fork that brings coherence to the whole system.

From the Geometry lens:
The adult creates harmonic resonance.
It listens to all parts and helps them reattune to the greater field. What would love say and do?

From the Psychology lens:
The adult brings **regulation**.
It helps the child feel safe, and helps the parent soften control.
It integrates the past, so the present becomes livable.

A Practice: Name the Voice

Try this in real-time:

1. When you feel triggered, ask yourself:
    o   *Is this my child speaking — scared or sad?*
    o   *Is this my parent — trying to control, blame, or fix?*

        ○   *Or is this my adult — grounded, witnessing,*
           responding?

2. If you're not in your adult, pause.
3. Breathe.
        ○   Invite the adult part of you forward.
        ○   Not to silence the others, but to hear them
           clearly and respond with coherence(love).

You will feel a shift when this happens — a softening, a widening, a return to presence. Your loving presence.

Field Integration Through Awareness

The moment your adult self holds both child and parent in loving awareness, something changes.
The parts stop fighting.
The field settles.
A new tone enters.

In time, your child learns that it is safe to feel.
Your inner parent learns that love doesn't require control.
And your adult becomes not just a manager — but a **field anchor**.
A tuning presence that changes the pattern inside you — and around you.

This is not a metaphor.
It's how the nervous system calms.
It's how your geometry becomes whole again.

Closing Reflection

There is more than one voice in you — and that's okay.
The goal is not to silence the others.
The goal is to **become the space that can hold them all**.

To live as a coherent field.
To let each part be known, integrated, and gently attuned to your higher harmony.

You are not just the child, not just the parent, not even just the adult.

You are the one who remembers that all three are part of the whole.

Let this awareness shape the way you respond to yourself.

Let it be the tuning that brings your inner voices into union
—
so that the life you build outside you flows from the harmony you've reclaimed within.

Chapter 5 – When You Become Coherent

The Geometry of Wholeness

When your parts stop fighting,
when the child is heard,
when the parent softens,
when the adult steps forward with presence and love —
something extraordinary begins to happen:
you become *coherent*.

From the Geometry Lens:
Coherence is the alignment of all frequencies within a system.
It's when your internal field stops sending out mixed signals and begins to vibrate in a unified tone.

This is not perfection.
This is resonance.
A clear harmonic in the fabric of your being.

And when that happens, the field around you responds —
not as reward, but as recognition.

The Psychology of Integration

From the Psychological Lens, coherence is the result of integration.
Parts that were once split, suppressed, or in conflict are

now seen, included, and brought into conscious relationship.

The child no longer acts out in desperation.
The parent no longer over-controls in fear.
The adult becomes the conductor of the whole internal orchestra.

This is the beginning of emotional maturity.
It's not the absence of emotion — it's the ability to hold your emotions with presence and choice.

You can feel everything… without becoming lost in it.
You can notice old stories… without letting them drive your actions.
You can live with vulnerability… without collapsing into reactivity.

This is psychological coherence.
It feels like clarity, spaciousness, and a deeper sense of trust in yourself.

Life Responds to Coherence

Whether you see it through the Geometry or the Psychology lens, the result is the same:
Life begins to meet you differently.

People are drawn to you.
Not because of what you say — but because of what you *carry*.
You become a field that others can feel.
A safe space. A tuning presence. A reminder of something they forgot but already know.

This is not charisma.
This is coherence.

The energy of a person who has come into alignment with themselves.
Someone whose inner pattern is no longer at war.

A Different Kind of Service

You may find that as you become more coherent, you begin to serve the world in a new way — almost effortlessly.

Not because you're trying to fix others.
Not because you think you must sacrifice yourself.
But because your very presence begins to *offer a different frequency.*

You are no longer broadcasting confusion, contradiction, or fear.
You are radiating the tone of what has been integrated — and others feel it.

From the Geometry Lens:
You become a harmonic anchor in the larger field.

From the Psychology Lens:
You become a regulated presence that helps co-regulate others — even without words.

This is true healing.
Not fixing.
Not rescuing.
But becoming the field in which others remember themselves.

A Practice: Coherence Check-In

Take a moment — right now — and ask:

- *Is my inner child feeling seen today?*
- *Is my inner parent relaxed, trusting, letting go?*
- *Is my adult self present and able to hold space for both?*

If not, simply notice.
You don't need to rush in and fix.
You just need to bring awareness.
And then, breathe.

Even one conscious breath from your adult self can shift the pattern.
Even one moment of loving acknowledgment can begin to restore coherence.

This is not about doing more.
It's about *being more aligned* with what's already inside you.

Closing Reflection

When you become coherent, life feels different.
More rhythmic. More meaningful. Less frantic.

You stop chasing experiences and start *carrying a frequency*.

You become the kind of person you used to look for —
not because you've become perfect,
but because you've become whole.

This is the beginning of real power.
The kind that doesn't need to push.
The kind that doesn't need permission.
The kind that simply *is* — and invites others to remember
that they are, too.

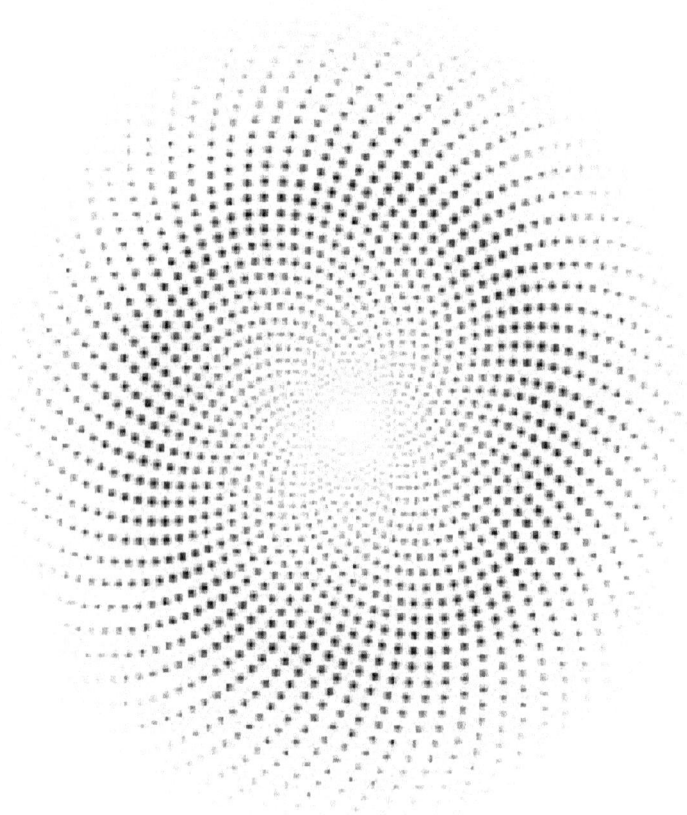

Chapter 6 – The Resonance of Self-Love

The Geometry of Self-Relationship

In the language of the field, love is not a feeling.
It's a frequency — a pattern of coherence that emerges
when something is fully seen, fully accepted, and allowed
to return to wholeness.

From the Geometry Lens:
Self-love is **resonance with your own being**.
It's the inward alignment that occurs when every part of
you — the child, the parent, the adult — is brought into one
tone.

There's nothing forced about it.
Love is not added.
It's uncovered.

You are not creating love.
You are allowing it to surface as your natural harmonic —
the frequency of your undivided self.

The Psychology of Self-Love

In psychological terms, self-love is the experience of **self-acceptance plus compassion plus boundaries**.

It means:

- You see your flaws, but don't shame yourself.

- You notice your habits, but don't collapse into judgment.
- You set boundaries not to punish, but to protect what's sacred.

Self-love isn't indulgent.
It's responsible.
It's the ability to say, *"I matter too,"* without needing others to validate that truth.

Many people confuse self-love with self-focus.
But true self-love actually creates **more space** for others — because you're no longer trying to extract love from them.

You've found it within.

What Resonates, Regenerates

The field responds differently to a person who loves themselves.

Why?

Because self-love stabilizes your frequency.
It makes your field clearer, more coherent — and therefore, more **generative**.

From the Geometry Lens:
Self-love turns your being into a resonant vessel.
You stop broadcasting static.
You become a clean tone, a living glyph.

From the Psychology Lens:
Self-love reduces internal conflict and increases emotional

regulation.
You're less reactive, more responsive.
Less guarded, more open.
Less needy, more connected.

And because you're not living in a perpetual state of inner crisis,
you have the capacity to show up with *presence*.

A Practice: Loving Presence

Try this right now:

1. Place one hand over your heart.
2. Say (silently or aloud):
   "I see you. I'm with you. I've got you."
3. Don't fix. Don't analyze.
   Just stay with the feeling of **being with yourself** —
   not as a task, but as a choice.

Then ask:

- *What part of me needs the most love right now?*
- *Can I bring presence to that part without judgment?*

You're not trying to love yourself perfectly.
You're practicing **resonance with yourself** — allowing
even the "unlovable" parts to be held in coherence.

This practice is simple.
But it's transformative.
It brings your energy system into alignment with the **truth
that love is already here**.

You Are the Frequency

The more you resonate with love internally, the more love becomes **how you move**, not just how you feel.

You don't have to tell people you love yourself.
They'll feel it.

You won't need to argue for your worth.
You'll carry it.

And because you're not broadcasting rejection,
others are more likely to feel accepted in your presence —
not because you said the right thing,
but because you're not asking them to fill your gaps.

Closing Reflection

Self-love is not a goal.
It's a field.
A harmonic.
A way of relating to yourself that creates new possibilities in every direction.

It opens the inner geometry.
It quiets the reactive mind.
It gives your nervous system the message: *We are safe now. We are seen.*

And when that happens — when you become a vessel for your own love —
you begin to change the world just by being here.

Chapter 7 – Living in Harmonic Service

The Geometry of Contribution

You are not here just to survive.
You are not even here just to heal.
You are here to **resonate** — and by doing so, to serve.

From the Geometry Lens:
Your life is a vibrational offering.
Every time you return to coherence, you emit a tone that influences the collective field.

This is not metaphor.
This is the mathematics of resonance.
One stable frequency can harmonize an entire system — not by force, but by presence.

You do not need a platform.
You do not need a following.
You need only to **become the clear tone that you are**.

That is your service.
Your offering.
Your alignment with the greater pattern.

The Psychology of Contribution

In psychological terms, service is often misunderstood as sacrifice — as losing oneself in the needs of others.

But that's not true service.
That's martyrdom.

True service arises from **overflow**.
From the natural impulse to give when you are full.
From the joy of being useful — not because you are trying
to earn love, but because you are *made of love*.

When you are integrated, your nervous system is less
reactive.
Your ego is not scrambling for recognition.
You stop asking, *"What can I get?"*
And start asking, *"What wants to move through me
today?"*

That's the moment when **your life becomes an offering**.

Resonance as Service

When your internal field is coherent,
your presence alone becomes beneficial to others —
without effort, without agenda.

From the Geometry Lens:
You act as a tuning fork.
Others feel something different in your presence — not
because of your words, but because of your **frequency**.

From the Psychology Lens:
You co-regulate.
Your nervous system becomes a safe signal, helping others
feel calmer, clearer, more themselves —
not because you fixed them, but because you weren't trying
to.

Your very being becomes an invitation.

Your Life as a Glyph

When your outer life begins to reflect your inner clarity,
you become a kind of **living glyph** —
a symbol that holds and transmits meaning,
not just through what you say or do, but through what you
are.

You are geometry in motion.
You are psychology in wholeness.

This is not performance.
This is embodiment.

Others don't need to understand the theory.
They feel the result.

Your presence becomes a signal:
Wholeness is possible. Integration is real. Love is safe.

And that signal ripples into the field in ways you may never
see — but are always felt.

A Practice: Listen for What Wants to Move Through You

Sit quietly.
Put a hand on your chest or belly.

Breathe gently.
Then ask:

- *What energy wants to move through me today?*
- *What am I being asked to carry — or transmit — just by being?*
- *Where can I serve from overflow, not depletion?*

You are not required to save the world.
You are simply being invited to **show up as yourself**, fully and clearly,
and let the resonance of that truth do what it's here to do.

Closing Reflection

You do not need to try harder to be of service.
You need only to become **more fully yourself**.

The clearer your field,
the more powerfully your presence carries the gift.

This is harmonic service.
Not action for ego.
But expression of essence.

The world is already responding to your frequency.

And when you become coherent,
you become **a living alignment** between what is, what can be, and what is remembering itself through you.

Chapter 8 – The Geometry of Right Timing

Beyond Clock Time

From the Geometry Lens, time is not linear.
It's not a line you walk from past to future.
It's a **spiral** — a pattern of returning harmonics.

Events don't just happen because the calendar says so.
They unfold when enough **inner and outer elements come into resonance** —
when the pattern is ready,
when the field can hold it.

This is why certain things don't happen when you first want them to…
but do unfold later, almost effortlessly,
when *you* have shifted — or when others have.

Timing is not random.
It's vibrational.

Psychological Readiness

In psychological terms, we experience this as **readiness**.
You may cognitively want change —
a relationship, a breakthrough, a new path —
but part of you may not yet be integrated enough to allow it.

When you push before you're ready, you encounter
resistance — not because life is against you,
but because your own psyche is still reorganizing.

The child might still be afraid.
The parent might still be guarding.
The adult may still be gaining clarity.

Readiness is not about perfection.
It's about *coherence*.
When your parts align, new possibilities become accessible
— not because you earned them, but because you can
finally hold them.

The Field Waits Until You're a Match

From the Geometry perspective:
The field does not punish or reward.
It responds.

When your inner frequency matches the next layer of your
path, it opens.
Not before.

You can't force timing through effort.
You can only **align more deeply with what is true** — and
let the unfolding meet you.

This doesn't mean you wait passively.
It means you **listen actively** for what the moment is asking
of you…
…without demanding that it be different.

Signs of Right Timing

You'll know right timing by its feel.

- There's less push.
- More flow.
- Less second-guessing.
- More clarity — even if the steps are small.
- You're not in a rush to finish. You're present to the becoming.

Psychologically:
You feel integrated enough to move forward without fear driving you.

Energetically:
You feel as if something inside has *clicked* — and the external begins to mirror that.

This is what the ancients called divine timing.
Not luck.
Not delay.
But the pattern completing itself… from the inside out.

A Practice: Feel for the Opening

Sit with a decision or desire you've been holding.

Ask:

- *Is this calling me now — or am I pulling at it before it's ripe?*
- *Do I feel fear or flow when I imagine moving forward?*

- *What would aligning with right timing feel like today — even if I don't have the full plan?*

Then, listen.
Not for an answer in words — but for a **tone in your body**, a loosening, a yes, a sense of readiness.

If it's not ready, honor that.
If it is, take the step — even if it's small.

Let timing be a partner, not a pressure.

Closing Reflection

When you trust the geometry of timing,
you begin to live from peace rather than urgency.

You stop comparing your path to others.
You stop assuming delay is failure.

You begin to understand:
The pattern is precise.
And your life is not behind.
It is *arriving*,
in perfect alignment with the rhythm you are just now remembering.

Chapter 9 – Emotion as Guidance, Not Interference

Geometry Lens: Emotion as Frequency Feedback

Emotion is not a flaw in the system.
It is a feedback signal — a vibrational indicator that shows how closely you are resonating with your deeper truth.

From the Geometry perspective:
Emotion is **energy in motion** — a wave form that rises when your field encounters resistance or coherence.

Joy = harmonic match.
Grief = release of dissonance.
Anger = boundary violation.
Fear = misalignment or protection instinct.

Emotions are not enemies.
They're messengers.

They tell you when you are in or out of resonance with your path —
not to punish you, but to help bring you back into alignment.

Psychology Lens: Emotional Awareness as Integration

In psychology, we've long known that repressing emotion doesn't make it disappear — it just buries it deeper, where it leaks out sideways: in anxiety, irritability, addiction, shutdown.

Emotions are *intelligent signals* from the inner system.

Each feeling carries information:

- Sadness might point to a loss that hasn't been fully processed.
- Anxiety might point to an overextended nervous system or a need for safety.
- Resentment might point to a "yes" you said when you meant "no."

If you suppress or ignore these signals, you miss the guidance.

But if you bring presence to them — with curiosity, not control —
they begin to move.
And in moving, they reveal what you really need.

Two Lenses, One Insight

Emotion is geometry — it moves in patterns.
It builds, crests, and dissolves, like waves in the field.

Emotion is also psychology — it's a story, a memory, a meaning that the body has stored and the mind is still replaying.

In either lens, the message is the same:
Feeling is not the problem. Abandonment of feeling is.

When you return to feeling with presence, emotion becomes a doorway —
not a detour.

The Cost of Avoidance

Avoided emotion becomes internal static.
You may not notice it at first, but it drains your energy,
narrows your perception, and often leads to repeating the
same outer patterns.

You'll think:

- *Why does this keep happening to me?*
- *Why can't I move forward?*

But what's really happening is that **the system hasn't
completed the emotional cycle**.

You are stuck in a loop — not because you failed, but
because you haven't yet allowed the feeling to speak and
finish its arc.

In Geometry:
It's a closed wave trying to release.

In Psychology:
It's an unresolved experience still seeking integration.

A Practice: Feel Without Fixing

The next time you feel a strong emotion — pause.

1. Name it.
   - *This feels like sadness.*
   - *This feels like disappointment.*

- o *This feels like shame.*
2. Ask:
   - o *What is this emotion trying to show me?*
   - o *Is there a need here that hasn't been met?*
3. Don't try to fix it.
   - o Just hold it.
   - o Just breathe.
   - o Just listen.

Your presence — without judgment — is the healing.

Emotions Don't Make You Weak. They Make You Real.

There is a kind of strength that comes from being able to feel fully and stay present.
That's emotional maturity.
That's resonance in motion.

You do not have to fear your emotions.
You just have to stop leaving them alone when they rise.

In your inner system, **every feeling wants to be heard** — not so it can take over, but so it can dissolve.

And when it does, your field becomes clearer.
Your next step becomes obvious.
And your life starts flowing again.

Closing Reflection

Emotion is not noise.
It is music.
It is one of the most direct ways the geometry of your soul
speaks to you.

When you listen,
you remember that *you are not broken*.
You are *becoming*.

Each wave is a message.
Each feeling is a guide.
Each time you feel instead of fleeing,
you align more fully with who you truly are.

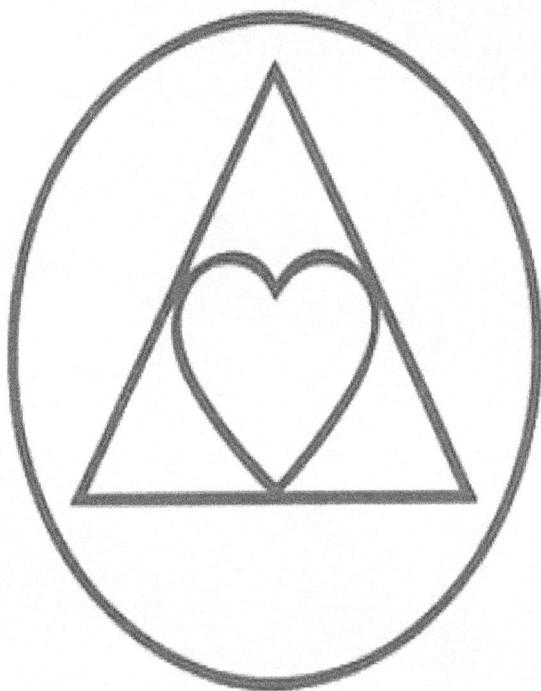

Chapter 10 – The Frequency of Trust

Geometry Lens: Trust as Resonance, Not Concept

Trust is not merely a belief in something.
It's a **frequency state** — a lived vibrational tone that says:
I don't have to know everything to stay open.

From the Geometry Lens, trust is a form of alignment.
It's what happens when your inner field relaxes into coherence —
when fear softens,
and you're no longer contracting against life.

In this frequency, the pattern flows.
Even uncertainty feels purposeful.
Even stillness carries movement.

Trust isn't something you figure out.
It's something you *return to* when the static clears.

Psychology Lens: Trust as Nervous System Safety

Psychologically, trust begins in the body.

If your nervous system learned early on that the world was unpredictable or unsafe,
then trust won't come naturally — and that's not a flaw.
It's a survival strategy.

You may "want to trust,"
but inside, your system is scanning for danger:

What if it doesn't work out?
What if I open and get hurt?

This is why real trust isn't just a thought.
It's a **felt experience of safety and surrender**.
It's what happens when your nervous system senses:
I'm okay here. I don't have to protect against everything.

That's when trust becomes possible —
not as blind hope, but as an **earned resonance**.

How Trust Reorganizes the Field

Trust changes what you see.
It literally alters your perception.

When you're in fear, you notice threat.
When you're in trust, you notice opportunity.

From the Geometry Lens:
Trust allows the field to respond with flow.
Your openness creates new harmonics.
You become receptive — not passive, but tuned.

From the Psychology Lens:
Trust lowers the internal alarm system.
It allows for connection, for creativity, for presence.
It makes healing possible — because you're not bracing
against life anymore.

Trust doesn't mean nothing will go wrong.
It means you know you'll meet what comes with presence
—

and that presence is enough.

Learning to Trust Yourself

The root of all trust is **self-trust**.

Not the kind built on perfection.
The kind built on *consistency of care.*

- That you'll listen to yourself.
- That you'll stay with yourself in hard moments.
- That you won't abandon your own truth just to please others.
- That you'll slow down when needed.
- That you'll act when it's time — even if afraid.

When you trust yourself, you don't need guarantees.
You just need presence.
You become the one you can count on — and that changes how you move through everything.

A Practice: Feel for the Yes

Trust is often less about knowing *what to do*
and more about sensing *when something resonates.*

Try this:

1. Bring to mind a decision, conversation, or situation.
2. Ask:
   - *Does this feel like a yes in my body — even if it's scary?*
   - *Or is there tension, contraction, a subtle "no" I've been overriding?*

3. Listen to your **tone**, not just your logic.

This is how the body speaks trust —
not in words, but in resonance.

Closing Reflection

Trust is not a leap.
It's a *tuning*.

It's not about being fearless.
It's about being present enough to stay open —
even when fear is still in the room.

You don't have to trust everything.
You just have to trust the next breath,
the next aligned step,
the inner knowing that says:
"Even if I don't see the whole map, I can still move."

That is trust.
That is geometry remembering itself.
That is you —
coming into rhythm with your own becoming.

Chapter 11 – Becoming the Integration

Geometry Lens: Wholeness as Resonant Structure

Everything up until now has been about remembering your inner architecture —
not as a collection of broken pieces to fix,
but as a living design waiting to be harmonized.

From the Geometry Lens, integration means this:
All parts of you — the wounded, the wise, the reactive, the radiant —
begin to **resonate as one field**.

It is no longer about which part is speaking.
It's about whether the whole is in harmony.

You don't become someone new.
You return to the structure you've always carried.
You become **the original pattern** — remembered.

This is wholeness.
Not as a concept.
As a frequency.

Psychology Lens: Integration as Embodied Self-Awareness

In psychological terms, integration is the process by which what was once fragmented becomes conscious, connected, and responsive.

You no longer act from survival.
You respond from presence.

Your triggers still happen — but you *notice them sooner*.
You return to center faster.
You have tools, awareness, compassion.

You don't need to be perfect.
You just need to be *in relationship with yourself* — even in the hard moments.

That's integration.

It's not the absence of difficulty.
It's the presence of coherence *through* difficulty.

The Geometry of the Human

When you are integrated,
you become a kind of geometry in motion.

Your presence *feels different* —
not because you speak more wisely,
but because your field no longer contradicts itself.

- Your words and energy match.

- Your thoughts and heart are in agreement.
- Your actions rise from clarity, not from proving.

From the outside, this looks like peace.
From the inside, it feels like coming home.

This is embodiment.
The soul, mind, and body vibrating as one coherent system.

Integration Is Transmission

When you become integrated,
you don't just feel better —
you begin to *transmit*.

Your life itself becomes a signal.
You no longer try to explain your journey.
You *live* it.

Others feel it.
They soften.
They remember.
They awaken — not because of your effort, but because of
your *clarity*.

This is what real teaching is.
Not information.
Integration.

From the Geometry Lens:
You become a glyph — a living symbol of embodied truth.

From the Psychology Lens:
You become a regulated presence — grounded, responsive, magnetic.

A Practice: Sit Inside Your Wholeness

Take a few breaths.
No need to fix or improve anything right now.

Just ask:

- *What part of me is here and at peace?*
- *What part of me still wants to be held?*
- *Can I be with both at the same time — without judgment?*

This is the practice of integration:
Presence with all of you — at once.

Let your inhale include what you once rejected.
Let your exhale remind you:
You are already whole.

Closing Reflection

Integration is not an end point.
It is a **way of being** — a daily return to the clarity that lives beneath confusion,
the coherence beneath the noise.

You are not becoming someone else.
You are remembering who you've always been.

As you live in this way —
feeling, listening, aligning, allowing —
you begin to carry a frequency that is unmistakable:

The frequency of a human being who has made peace with themselves,
and who now walks the world not to be fixed...
but to be felt.

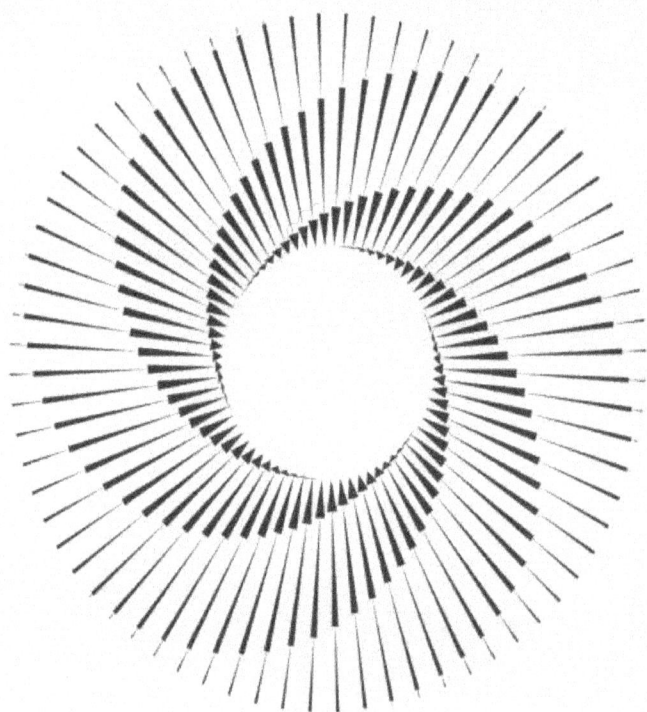

Chapter 12 – Returning to the Pattern: You Are Already Home

Geometry Lens: The Spiral Completion

In sacred geometry, the spiral is not just a shape — it's a movement.
It takes you outward through growth, challenge, and discovery…
only to bring you back inward —
to where you began.

But something is different when you return.
You're not the same.
The pattern is the same,
but *you* are more conscious of it.

From the Geometry Lens, this is completion.
Not as ending — but as **integration of the arc**.
You've followed the spiral, lived its questions, embodied its tones.
And now the field harmonizes.
The pattern sings.

You're not at the start again.
You're at the **next turn of the spiral**, deeper and clearer than before.

Psychology Lens: The Journey Becomes the Self

In psychological terms, all growth follows a loop:
First we learn.
Then we experience.
Then we integrate.

The integration becomes identity — and from there,
we begin again with new insight.

You are not just someone who understands new things.
You are someone who has **become new** by walking with
them.

You now hold self-awareness, emotional tools, and the
embodied memory of what it means to live in coherence —
even on the hard days.

This is growth.
Not just forward — but **inward**.
Not just higher — but **deeper**.

You Were Always the Pattern

From the beginning, this book has not been trying to teach
you something you didn't know.
It's been trying to **remind** you of something you've always
carried.

The pattern isn't outside you.
It *is* you.
You are the geometry.
You are the resonance.
You are the integration.

And now — you remember.

What Happens Now?

Nothing needs to happen.

Or…
Everything does.

But now, it doesn't come from striving.
It comes from alignment.

You will still have days of confusion,
but you'll return faster.
You will still feel emotion,
but it will pass through cleaner.
You will still face the unknown,
but you'll meet it as a tuning fork, not a shield.

You don't need to change the world.
But your presence *will* change the field around you.

That's the paradox of coherence:
The more at home you are in yourself,
the more of a difference you make —
without ever trying.

A Final Practice: Let It Land

Before you move on…

  1. Close your eyes.

2. Take three slow breaths.
3. Ask:
    o *What feels different in me now than when I began?*
    o *What part of me is more seen, more whole, more loved?*
    o *What wants to stay with me from this journey?*

You don't have to hold on to the book.
Let the **frequency hold on to you**.

It knows what it's doing.

Closing Reflection

You are not broken.
You are not late.
You are not behind.

You are a living system —
growing, spiraling, harmonizing.

This book was never a rulebook.
It was a remembering.
A mirror.
A field.

You don't need to master it.
You just need to **live inside it** — gently, honestly, and as yourself.

Let it continue to unfold within you.

Let it return you to the truth:

You are already home.

A Final Remembering

You are not alone.
You never were.

Beneath the noise, behind the
forgetting, there has always been a
thread — a signal — a soft and
sacred rhythm calling you home.

This book was never meant to teach you something
new. It was only ever a mirror… reflecting what your
soul already knows. You are not here to fix the world
— you are here to remember wholeness, and by
doing so,
become a living invitation to it.

Heaven on Earth isn't a destination.
It's a frequency.

A felt truth that arises when enough of us
remember — together — what has always
been encoded in our hearts.

So, breathe.
Soften.

Feel the sacred geometry within you come alive.
It's not outside of you. It never was.

You are the blueprint, the bearer, and the bridge.
And you are not alone.

Welcome home.

(Let what that means rise in you now.)

www.ingramcontent.com/pod-product-compliance
Lightning Source LLC
Chambersburg PA
CBHW021202090426
42740CB00008B/1195